I0065563

MASTERING MEETINGS
THAT MATTER
8 Essentials for Making Your Meetings More Productive

Gavin Grift, Colin Sloper & Heather De Blasio

A catalogue record for this book is available from the National Library of Australia

Copyright © 2023 Grift Education. All rights reserved.

This work is copyright. Apart from fair dealings for the purposes of study, research, criticism or review, or as permitted under the Copyright Act 1968 (Cth), no part should be reproduced, transmitted, communicated or recorded, in any form or by any means, without the prior written permission of the copyright owner.

grifteducation
Empowering Educators

Publisher:
Inspiring Publishers
P.O. Box 159, Calwell, ACT Australia 2905
Email: publishaspg@gmail.com
http://www.inspiringpublishers.com

National Library of Australia Cataloguing-in-Publication entry

Authors: Gavin Grift, Colin Sloper & Heather De Blasio

Title: **Mastering Meetings That Matter:**
   8 Essentials for Making your Meetings more Productive

ISBN: 978-1-922920-17-1 (Print)
ISBN: 978-1-922920-18-8 (eBook)

Foreward

As you hold this book in your hands, the title says it all. Time is a most valuable resource, and we cannot afford to waste it on unproductive meetings that don't matter; that don't make a difference to the students and educators we serve.

So, to use this precious time wisely, read on to find out how you can transform the way you approach meetings where the privilege of sharing time with others can be used to create positive change. With this book, you'll gain practical insights into how to make meetings impactful and productive, build highly effective teams, and achieve outcomes that only occur when people truly work together.

The authors are well-known for their ability to turn theory into practice and have done so in the development of this valuable resource to help educators make the most of every minute when meeting. They emphasise the importance of bringing people together to work interdependently to strengthen their impact with and for one another. This makes *Mastering Meetings that Matter* a must-read for any leader looking to increase the impact of their collaborative endeavours with a focus on learning for all.

The 8 essentials to making meetings more productive are informed by the rich lived experience of the authors grounded in relevant and contemporary research and practice. Whether you are an experienced leader or just starting, this book is a powerful blend of helping educators with both the people and process aspects of leading meetings. The concept of mastering is apt, given the depth of thinking, ideas, and tools provided in the book to ensure it matters for all levels of leaders and those they lead.

This gem of a book is a perfect resource for educational leaders who want to make the most of every minute they spend in meetings with others. So, read on and discover how you can make your meetings, matter!

Dr Barbara Watterston
Chief Executive Officer
Australian Council for Educational Leaders (ACEL)

About Grift Education

Grift Education is an international professional learning provider for educators. We work with educators to design impactful learning experiences that support them to overcome the many challenges of their role, develop leadership identity, increase collaborative intelligence and strengthen the impact of their teaching.

Drawn from the extensive work and books of Grift Education founder Gavin Grift, our mission is to empower educators to take genuine charge of their own professional journey. Impacting from our actions, influencing others and increasing learning for all sits at the heart of this mission.

These services are ideal for educators:

- Looking for opportunities to enhance their impact
- Wanting to shine as a leader
- Struggling with the day-to-day pressure of their role
- Wondering how to improve their impact in the classroom and beyond
- Seeking to work more productively with their colleagues
- Interested in the most up-to-date teaching and leadership approaches.

Our seminars, webinars, online courses and in-person events are held regularly throughout the year, and you can find out more at www.grifteducation.com

About The Authors

Gavin Grift

Gavin Grift is the Founder and CEO of Grift Education. Gavin's passion, commitment, humour and highly engaging style have made him one of Australia's most in-demand presenters. Through his keynotes, seminars, and coaching services, Gavin connects with national and international audiences on how to cultivate authentic collaboration, build success in others and genuinely commit to reflective practice. His belief in the development of defined professional autonomy for educators both challenge and connect the head and heart of his audiences. As a leading Australian author, he has combined his beliefs, research and experiences on the importance of collaboration and coaching to co-author numerous books including 5 Ways of Being, Teachers as Architects of Learning, Transformative Talk, and Collaborative Teams That Work.

Colin Sloper

Colin Sloper is a leading expert and author on Professional Learning Communities. Colin works with systems, schools, leaders and educators to transform them into high-performing professional learning communities and build their capabilities to operate as members of highly effective collaborative teams. Colin's skills as an educational leader, speaker and coach – alongside his practical advice and knowledge as someone who has transformed schools – are highly sought after by educational organisations across all sectors. He is co-author of numerous books including Collaborative Teams That Work, Collaborative Systems of Support: Learning for All, Learning by Doing: A Handbook for Professional Learning Communities at Work® (Australian Edition) and Professional Learning Communities – Voices from the Field for Hawker Brownlow Education.

Heather De Blasio

Heather is co-author of the bestselling book, Five Ways of Being (Danvers, De Blasio & Grift, 2020), Mastering Meetings That Matter (Grift, Sloper, De Blasio, in print) and a contributing author to the second edition of Assessment for Teaching (Griffin ed., 2017).

A highly sought-after professional learning leader, Heather is renowned for her unique ability to authentically develop the leadership capacity of others. She works with leaders, directors and leadership teams across sectors and regions in Australia and internationally. In addition to her executive leadership work, Heather also delivers selected programs with Grift Education, and currently serves in a part-time capacity as the Director of Leadership and Human Potential at Wilderness School in Adelaide, South Australia.

Contents

About Grift Education 5

About The Authors 7

Dedication 11

Introduction 13

  1. Set the Scene 21

  2. Get clear 44

  3. Make it Relevant 56

  4. Build your Skills 71

  5. Foster Ownership 84

  6. Be on the Same Page 88

  7. Avoid Distractions 92

  8. Beware of Interuptions 96

Epilogue 100

Reference List 102

Dedication

This book is dedicated to anyone who has ever
uttered these words to themselves (or someone else)
after attending a meeting...

"There's an hour of my life I'll never get back."

Introduction

Eyerolling.
Yawning.
Surreptitious (or not-so-surreptitious) texting.
Boredom.
Disconnection.
Apathy.
Hopelessness.

Sound familiar?

How many times have we sat through meetings that seemed completely pointless - a meeting just for the sake of having a meeting?

Compressed or barely stifled resentment and hostility can simmer just below the surface, leaving participants feeling bored, defeated, unheard, invisible, or just plain sad. Faith in such meetings diminishes, as does our capacity to develop productive working relationships with our teams.

But what if we walked away from such meetings smiling, laughing or with a fresh spring in our step? What if we felt optimistic, supported, valued, heard, known and appreciated? And what if we felt accomplished, satisfied and connected to each other and our best selves, knowing that we are doing what really matters?

And what if we could harness the unique talents, skills, passions and capacity for contribution that sit in the hearts and minds of *all* participants?

You might wonder what that might look like or what it might take to get there. Who might you need to be, either as a leader or a team member in a school or educational organisation, to lead and participate in team meetings that really make a difference?

This handbook provides an antidote to the demotivating factors and the underwhelming outcomes of too many meetings that rob our schools, leaders and teachers of the opportunity to make a difference to students, each other – and ultimately, themselves.

We'll do this by taking a dual focus on the *doing* – that is 'what to do' in meetings – and the *being*, which boils down to 'who we need to be' in meetings. If we are to plan, facilitate and lead team meetings that draw us ever closer to our highest educational aspirations, both approaches are needed.

Meetings are vital in all organisations and schools. Indeed, depending on our positions or our organisation, we may spend a great deal of our time in meetings. At their best, meetings can inspire, create and strengthen connections, facilitate the carrying out of the right 'work' of the organisation, drive the operationalisation of the mission and strategic intents, lead to better decision making and improve both outcomes and impact.

Through exploring eight essentials for successful meetings, we present practical tasks and practices that can be implemented immediately and make a significant difference to the meeting itself, and its outcomes. Of course, for any meeting to be successful, you'll need to bring people along with you, and we'll also show you how to do this. We'll dive deep into how to take a holistic approach to these eight essentials, so that every meeting matters and makes a difference to participants.

Mastering meetings that matter...

Let's unpack that a little.

Mastering (verb): acquiring complete knowledge or skill or competence in something

Meetings (noun): an act or process of coming together

Matter (verb): meaning of significance, or consequence and importance to someone, carry weight, or make a difference.

We argue that, regardless of context, the kinds of meetings that truly make a difference and have the greatest impact are collaborative by nature. We are stronger when we act together, rather than as individuals, and the strength of our relationships with our team members ultimately shapes how well we can do the work.

The work of Garmston and Wellman (2013) provides us with an apt description of what constitutes a successful meeting, which we share here.

> Successful meetings "take minimum time, produce maximum work, and generate a maximum amount of member satisfaction. The ultimate goal is that meetings serve as vehicles to protect and support the primary mission of the school, which is student learning".
>
> *(pg. 74)*

This handbook focuses directly on the meetings of collaborative teams in schools, whether they be collaborative teams in a Professional Learning Community (PLC), year level teams, pastoral care teams, vertical teams or faculty/discipline-based/ curriculum teams. Through exploring eight essentials, we provide a guide for leaders and participants to develop their knowledge, skill and competence in leading and facilitating collaborative team meetings. The aim is for educators to be able to make a difference, by increasing their impact.

You might be thinking: a difference to, or impact on whom or what?

Simply put, the 'who' comprises all those who benefit from, or are impacted by, the work of the team and that particular meeting. For schools, which are by their very nature learning focused and devoted to fostering the learning and growth of others, those impacted by meetings will include both students *and* staff.

The 'what' is defined by the purpose for which the team has been created in the first place. As mentioned above, there are many types of teams created in schools and they are created for a variety of purposes. We would strongly argue that the closer a team's existence aligns to the fundamental purpose of a school (i.e. to achieve high levels of learning for all students) the more important the team's existence, and work is. We see collaborative teams in a PLC as the fundamental tool for improving student learning, but other teams also serve an important function in supporting the work of these engines of school improvement.

The purpose of this handbook is to help team leaders and members optimise the processes and outcomes of collaborative team meetings, so they can increase their capacity to maximise the learning of the students they serve.

But given that team meetings that matter can also make a difference to the meeting participants, it goes beyond this.

So how can this be? And what might that look like?

One way of looking at it is that meetings only matter to participants because of how the meeting makes them think, act and feel. When we master meetings that create impact, we are intentional about touching the hearts, minds and souls of our participants by engaging them in the 'right work', and deliberately fostering their growth and capacity to contribute in a meaningful way to the work we're committed to.

In truth, in any high-performing organisation or school, meetings can only matter if people are engaged in the 'right work'. But what is the right work?

It is critical that when collaborative teams meet, their meetings are tightly focused on the 'right work' – the work that will make a difference. For a team to come together for a meeting, there must be absolute urgency around the thought that, "we can't achieve the outcome we want unless we do the work collaboratively". There must be a genuine and important reason for people to give up their valuable time to attend. Indeed, if a meeting revolves around tasks that can be done independently or are for information sharing only, why is the meeting being called at all?

What constitutes the right work also depends on the underlying function and mission of the organisation, and the organisational level at which the meeting is taking place. In school leadership teams, the 'right work' may be defined as anything that advances the school's mission, the learning of students or the broad educational purpose of education, such as trying to unlock the full potential of everyone. In a pastoral team meeting, the right work might be centred on creating a learning environment where student wellbeing is supported and nurtured so that students can engage fully in their learning. In curriculum/subject discipline related meetings, the right work might be determining the key skills, knowledge and dispositions and the best ways to ensure students master these.

In our book *Collaborative Teams That Work* (Sloper & Grift, 2020), which focuses on the work of collaborative teams in high-performing PLCs, we clarify how educators work, the process they use and the desired outcome of their work. And when it comes to a PLC, we believe the definition of the 'right work' is guided by the desire to have team members working collaboratively - by using action research to inquire into and increase the impact of their actions.

This commitment is founded on the basic premise that as educators, we all want to improve the learning of our students, and we recognise that collaborative team meetings are the essential forum and vehicle for achieving this. In many ways this is no different to the premise that should inform most meetings in learning organisations such as schools, regardless of whether they are senior leadership team meetings, pastoral care meetings, curriculum meetings or finance meetings.

No matter what we're doing in any meeting, if we are to meet our highest goals, we want it to impact the learning of our students in some way. And we need to bear that goal in mind when preparing for, facilitating and participating in any meeting.

Who is this handbook for?

For school teams of all kinds and at all levels in the school hierarchy who are charged with the goal of leading learning in their organisation, and do this through their collaborative endeavours.

How to use it

There is no prescribed manner for progressing through the handbook, although the eight essentials are laid out in a logical sequence if you choose to tackle it that way.

The eight essentials of successful meetings

The eight essentials emerged from both our writing of *Collaborative Teams That Work* (Sloper & Grift, 2020), which is based on decades of research and work with schools across Australia, as well as our lived experiences as educators and observers of teams for over 10 years.

While these essentials provide powerful and practical strategies that can strengthen any meeting, at any level, conducted at any school, they should be applied to every collaborative team meeting within a PLC.

In this handbook, we'll look at what makes an effective team, what could be considered an effective meeting, and how to strengthen the meetings in your school - no matter what their purpose.

You'll be able to start using these strategies right away, leading to a direct benefit for both your students and colleagues.

So let's introduce each of the eight essentials.

1. **Set the scene**
   Ensure that all team members understand the team norms: who we are and how we work together
2. **Get clear**
   Ensure all team members are clear about their role
3. **Make it relevant**
   Ensure agenda items progress the team's purpose or goals
4. **Build your skills**
   Continue to strengthen meeting facilitation skills as we work through the agenda
5. **Foster ownership**
   Ensure agenda items for the subsequent meeting are developed collaboratively at the current meeting

6. Be on the same page
Ensure the actions agreed to at the meeting are clearly understood by all team members

7. Avoid distractions
Ensure non-essential items don't dominate the agenda

8. Beware the interruptions
Ensure all team members are informed of, and clear about, any events or school happenings that might impact on the meeting's actions.

As we explore these essentials in the following pages, we invite you to reflect on the following questions in order to clarify your next steps:

Where is your team in relation to this essential?

How are you facilitating this action?

What might you need to stop doing, continue doing or start doing?

How does your team need to show up to increase impact and what might this mean for you as facilitator?

1.

Set the Scene

Ensure that all team members understand the team norms: who we are and how we work together

To maximise the opportunity and capacity for teams to conduct meetings that achieve their purposes and desired outcomes (to really matter and make a difference to participants and those they serve), they must be set up for success.

It's vital for teams and team members to understand that the disciplined collaboration they undertake at meetings - from the deliberate use of discussion and dialogue to the way team members interact and respond to one another - is different to how they may interact in a more social context. It's also different to how they interact with each other during their daily work.

Given the nature of the disciplined collaboration they must undertake, and that teams are made up of people with uniquely individual personalities and behaviours, there needs to be explicit agreements within the group regarding who we are with each other and how we work together. These can be called ground rules, working agreements or, as we prefer, team norms.

Team norms provide a set of rules of engagement for the team. They express explicit guidelines and agreement on the behaviours that all team members need to exhibit (and those that should not be exhibited) for all team members to feel safe and comfortable participating wholeheartedly.

At their best, team norms provide the foundation for a positive team culture, one in which every team member feels comfortable and safe to maximise their contribution to whatever work or activities the team needs to do.

So, when it comes to working as a collaborative team, what are your team norms?

Defining your team's norms

Not so familiar with norms?

Norms are the professional behaviour standards to which all team members agree to commit. Defining them should be one of the very first tasks undertaken by a team. So, when a new team is formed – perhaps at the beginning of the year, or when a team is formed for a short-term project - the team should spend some time clearly articulating the behaviours that will support the achievement of their collaborative endeavours, and those that won't. In other words, what are the behaviours that we're going to accept, and what behaviours are not acceptable in our meetings?

Quite often when we talk about norms in our work with schools, teams tell us: "Oh, we are nice people. We don't really need norms because we're polite and we're courteous. We have good social skills."

And while this may be true in terms of how they generally interact with each other on a professional or day-to-day level, team meetings are different because they require disciplined collaboration.

Team norms can also create a safe and trusting culture for team members if unhealthy conflict surfaces, or may even prevent things escalating in the first place. They engender trust and safety for team members, particularly when emotions get heightened. This is especially true given many educators are so passionate about their work. Their sense of self-worth may very well be tied up in their identity as an educator, particularly for the many educators who still see teaching as a 'calling' of the highest order. They may hold very dearly to certain beliefs and practices and feel threatened if their deeply held values are challenged in a team meeting.

If it's a collaborative team meeting in the true sense of a PLC, and the discussions are laser focused on teaching practice, we know from experience that all teachers hold the way they teach very close to their heart. It is when teams start to have these rigorous discussions about the impact of their teaching practice that the need for norms really surfaces. In less challenging discussions about less significant tasks, the need for norms is less obvious or important. However, without team norms, if a team starts to flounder into dysfunctional patterns of behaviours, it is much harder to restore the team to healthy and respectful ways of working together.

Indeed, the purpose of any school team where collaboration underpins the work is not for everyone to agree with each other – it's to generate new solutions to the problems that the team is investigating. For this to happen, there must be rigour and disagreements in the discussions. People should be encouraged to argue their point and put their views forward. We want rigorous and passionate discussion, and even what might be called graceful disagreement, because that's how new ideas are surfaced and shaped.

It's important to raise the quality and rigour of these discussions by first articulating what the accepted meeting behaviours are so that people feel safe to have their say. The norms create the culture that allows the team to reap the benefits that true collaboration provides.

However, some of you may have had negative experiences of team norms. You may not have seen their value or resented the time taken to create them. They may have been created in a climate of optimism and then subsequently been forgotten and never revisited. Or they may have been used in an unkind way or as a form of social control.

While acknowledging the reality of these experiences, we are convinced that to master meetings that truly matter and have an impact on those who participate and benefit from the team's work, strong norms are paramount. Teams that allocate time to talk about who they are as a team and who they need to show up as, both individually and collectively, set themselves up for success. Of course, there also needs to be time allocated for regular reflection on how well the norms are serving the team's purpose and supporting the growth of the team's collaborative expertise.

For those who might argue that this all takes time and time away from our real work, we propose that sometimes in education we need to take time to save time. We take time while things are smooth to establish these shared agreements, so that when the seas get rough, we have a guiding compass to take us safely home. This means that we don't have to suddenly establish the behaviour expectations when we are under duress or heightened stress or emotion. Without agreed upon and lived team norms, if a team starts to flounder into dysfunctional patterns of behaviours, it is also much harder to restore the team to healthy and respectful ways of working together.

Fortunately, it's never too late to create norms, or for them to begin to have a positive impact, no matter how long your team has existed!

What to consider when deciding on your norms

For team norms to be anything more than lip service, or a set of noble principles that are created then put in a file and promptly forgotten, all team members need to be involved in their creation. This means that the team facilitator must carefully plan how to involve all members in the process, by choosing protocols and routines that ensure equal participation. All voices must be heard, and there must be collective agreement on how a final decision is made. We also recommend keeping the team norm list short and memorable to ensure that there is clarity and a shared understanding. This only comes through explicit dialogue about what each team member understands by each norm, then a discussion where the team members reach agreement regarding what is demanded by each norm. Ambiguity and imprecision are the enemies of effective norms.

In developing your team norms, we suggest you consider the following questions:

What behaviours currently impede the productivity and impact of the team? If the team has worked together previously, or some of the members have been on a project together, are there any behaviours that have been observed previously that might have a detrimental impact on your productivity – both in terms of outcomes for your students and each team member? For example, you may have sometimes run short of time because you spent an exorbitant amount of time discussing the wrong issues or members of the team consistently turned up late.

We know teachers are time poor. So the aim is to make sure, through acknowledgement of these behaviours, that when teams do meet that team members are as productive as possible, and use every second of the meeting to progress the work they want to do together.

What behaviours might strengthen the productivity in the impact of the team? Make sure you identify these. For example, in some teams we've worked with, they've asked at the meeting: what behaviours really assisted us in our work together? By doing this, you consciously reflect on a lived experience, not only whether you achieved the outcomes you wanted and whether you did it in the most effective and purposeful way.

These two overarching questions are of critical importance to the work the team needs to accomplish and address the 'what we do' or 'what I do' part of team meetings. For team meetings to truly matter - to make a difference to both team members and the end-product of the work they do together - we argue that teams also need to consider the 'who I am' and 'who does my team need me to be' type questions. Through this lens team members are more likely to intimately explore their personal needs and the things they need to be mindful of to support the team's disciplined collaboration.

Without this exploration and consideration of the 'being' side of collaborative team meetings, we run the risk of ignoring the heart and soul side of the individuals that make up the team. Ignoring their essential humanity sends an implicit message that who you are as an individual is not important: it is only what you do. This reduces our team members and our colleagues to impersonal, deindividualised cogs in an institutional machine. This kind of mentality should have been banished with the end of the first industrial revolution and yet it still exists, to the detriment of our schools, students, teachers, and our communities.

In our work *Five Ways of Being* (Danvers, De Blasio and Grift, 2020), we recognise that teachers and leaders bring their whole human selves to school, complete with unique human experiences and a rich tapestry of influences. These include layers of individual emotional intelligence, personality, current skill and ability levels, and our cultural and formative influences and experiences of power (Aguilar, 2016). These should all be closely considering during the process of creating norms.

Along with the two questions above, and to ensure our whole human selves are considered in the norm creation process, we suggest teams also consider the following question:

- **What behaviours and practices does each team member need to exhibit to contribute as their best self**?

Now it may be that what emerges here will not suit everyone. But it's likely that the process of exploring these more human aspects of the team's ways of working in meetings will surface important knowledge and insights for all team members to be more aware of. As a result, they can respect each other's individuality – not just their team membership role. It's also likely that members can reach agreement on which norms they can commit to in this realm, leading to greater harmony and caring in the team.

Be aware that when facilitating the exploration of such deeply personal territory, team members are asked to show their vulnerability. This can strengthen the team's understanding of individual team member's perceptions and also fosters respect and empathy towards one another. We do need, however, to be sensitive to individual team members' levels of comfort, concern and openness to sharing in this way as this might be something quite new and challenging for some.

In Keys to Successful Meetings (Hirsh et. Al, 1994) the authors first introduced us to six categories that can be useful in forming norms that are valuable for teams. They are:

Time: What rules and behaviours will we set around time, to make the time spent at meetings as effective as possible?

Listening: How are we going to make sure we're listening to each other? What behaviours does our team need to commit to and be aware of to make sure we're listening to the contributions of other people, rather than being individuals primarily focusing on our own ideas?

Confidentiality: Which issues at the meeting are confidential, and which can be shared outside the meeting? It's important to make sure your team has real clarity on this.

Decision making: As a team, how are we going to make decisions? And once a decision has been reached, how will all team members ensure that decision is carried out?

Participation: How will our team ensure there is equal participation from all members? How will we make sure that everyone feels like they've had the opportunity to express their point of view and be heard?

Expectations: If any behaviours don't fit into the categories above, they might fall under the area of general expectations.

It's also critically important for the team to unpack each norm into the specific behaviours that will or won't be demonstrated, so that there is clarity for all team members over what that norm might look, sound and feel like. This way there is no misunderstanding of what the norm is requiring of them at the meeting. Clarity means problematic behaviours, which can impede the team's effectiveness, will be reduced or hopefully eliminated. By naming the behaviours we might expect to see, and agreeing on such definitions, we also come to 'know' them and can choose these specific behaviours more successfully and intentionally.

Unpacking an example

Let's say a team comes up with a norm about listening. For example, that all team members will actively and respectfully listen to each other.

While this is a great start, for this norm to be effective and lived as part of the team culture and practice, your team members really need to drill down into and spell out the specific behaviours that this norm demands.

For example, we might agree to show that we are actively and respectively listening by using Post-it notes when we think of something that we want to add to the meeting, but want to avoid interrupting the flow. And we might agree not to interrupt when a person is presenting or speaking. Or it might be that team members agree to use positive body language, which is spelt out further as direct eye contact, nodding, open stances, leaning forward, and giving their full attention to the speaker.

Another norm might focus on team members agreeing to adopt the mindset of seeking to understand, rather than seeking to be understood at each meeting. For example, as a team member is speaking, the group might consciously ask themselves: "What does this person mean?" or "what are the implications of what this person is saying?" Rather than interrupting the speaker, they agree to use paraphrasing and ask questions to clarify meaning at the appropriate time, and commit to focusing discussions on the agenda item, rather than getting side-tracked.

It is important to note that other teams in the school might have the same norm, but their specific behaviour commitments may be completely different as they respond to different team members' personalities, current levels of collaborative expertise and the actual agenda or focus of their team.

Include the team norms on the agenda

It should be standard meeting practice and part of the meeting agenda template for team norms to be listed on each agenda. The listing of norms provides a reference point and a reminder to all team members of the behaviour commitments made to each another, ensuring their collaborative endeavours at each meeting are as effective as possible.

The reason we include norms on the agenda (or at least a summary) is to make sure they are always visible to team members. These visual reminders remind team members of how important these team norms are to their success – both in terms of the outcomes of their work together, and in strengthening how the team works together collaboratively to maximise the contribution and commitment of each team member. In this way, if there happens to be a lapse or someone has forgotten what the norms are, team members can refer back to the agenda and remind each other of what rules of engagement they've agreed to.

Ensure that there is at least one focus norm

At the start of any meeting, it's important to highlight the norm the team should be focusing on. This norm will have been identified as an area the team might have struggled with or could improve on at the previous meeting, or one that will be important to be conscious of to guide the team in the specific work they are undertaking in that meeting. Let's say, for example, that during the previous meeting, the norm observer reported back: "We did really well in keeping to the allocated time for each agenda item but during some of the discussions many people got very excited and were talking over each other".

This identified behaviour then becomes the focus norm for the subsequent meeting, which should begin with the norm observer saying something like: "Hey, at the last meeting we noticed we were talking over each other. What are some things we can do at this meeting to make sure that doesn't happen today?" Allow time for the brainstorming and sharing of ideas. Ask: "What might each of us need to be particularly conscious of in order to ensure our collective and individual behaviours align with that norm?" Allow time for reflection and public sharing – as this builds commitment to success. Once this has been clarified the meeting proper can commence by stating, "Now that we are clear on our focus norm, let's start our work."

At the end of the meeting, the team can then review whether any of the implemented suggestions have resulted in an improvement in the team's collaborative functioning. And indeed, everyone can reflect on how well they met their intention to be particularly conscious of something that would support the greater adherence to the focused norm.

When used well, team norms are a vital tool in mastering team meetings that really matter.

Make sure norms aren't imposed

The creation of norms is not the job of the team leader. A team leader should not, for example, declare: "Here's what I have observed in the meeting. Here are the behaviours everyone's doing wrong, and here's our new norms!"

Rather, team members must 'own' and commit to the norms. So, the process used to develop norms must harness and support the collaborative nature of the work the team will undertake – preferably early in the piece. If it's a grade level team or a subject level team, the first meeting of the year is an ideal time to establish and reach agreement on the norms that the team will follow.

A whole-school approach

While individual teams within schools will often generate their own norms, sometimes an entire school will also have a common set of norms for all meetings.

For example, we recently conducted a whole-school meetings process with a school. At a staff meeting, participants generated the norms for all team meetings. For each norm developed, they listed the specific behaviour commitments to make each norm as clear and specific as possible. This process allowed all participants to have input and ownership of the norms, as well as the more specific behaviour requirements.

These norms and commitments were then printed and copied on to large posters, which were displayed prominently in all the school's meeting areas. This created a visual reminder to staff that these were the behaviour commitments expected to ensure all meetings were purposeful and effective. It also supported the building of a truly collaborative culture, which expresses the commitment of the school to acknowledge and care for each individual teacher, and to ensure there are rules in place to make this commitment more likely. Doing something like this makes a very public statement about who we are as a school and what is important to us, which is our people. It's not just about the work we all do together. It's that we are prepared to take the time to put in place formal measures to safeguard the psychological safety and wellbeing of all our people while we do our shared work.

No matter what approach is taken, it's important to remember that norms and behaviour commitments do not exist as an end in themselves. They help establish the necessary conditions to allow the highest possible level of collaboration by having school personnel consciously consider the culture required to be successful in their team endeavours.

How to get reluctant staff members on board

One of the biggest challenges we come across with educators who are wanting to elevate their collaborative efforts is managing to get everybody united, or 'on the bus'.

Consider the following questions: What do you do for the staff member who seems resentful of the collaborative process? What do you do for the staff member who doesn't engage or adhere to the team norms, even when they have had a voice in creating them?

These are challenging but important questions. We do not believe that any of us wakes up in the morning and says: "Oh, I can't wait for today's meeting and to embrace a bit of conflict today". But the truth is that if we don't put something in place, and if we don't build a common language for how we're going to build effective behaviours in meetings, then these unprofessional behaviours will continue to be ignored, threatening the achievement of the outcomes we're trying to accomplish by working together.

So how does a team deal with the situation where norms are being broken, or breached?

Rules are made to be broken

It's important for teams to recognise and even anticipate that norms will be broken. We are human after all; we are not unfeeling impersonal machines. If we create the meeting culture for rigorous conversations to thrive, it means norms will get broken as people get used to working using disciplined collaboration.

However as members gain a growing understand that the way they interact at a meeting is different from a social situation, breaches of the norms will become less frequent.

Anticipating that norms will be broken and establishing a breach procedure from the very start, and prior to any such occurrence, ensures the way breaches are responded to doesn't become personal. Instead, it becomes a professional response because it's something already agreed on as a team. We can then identify and gently challenge the behaviour in a non-confrontational manner with something like ... "Hey everyone, remember that this isn't personal. It's just the process that we agreed to go through when this occurs".

So how can we ensure that all team members commit to and follow the team norms?

Remember that when team norms are developed, teams consider specific questions such as:

- What behaviours are unacceptable?
- What behaviours might undermine our endeavours?
- What might get in the way of achieving our desired outcomes?
- What behaviours and practices might need to be exhibited so we can each contribute as our best selves?

An important follow-up question for teams to consider when norms are being developed is: "What are we going to do when our norms are broken?" A great starting point for this discussion is to explore team members' responses and come to a shared agreement in response to the question: "How would you like to be treated if you are the one who has broken the norm?"

The breach procedure needs to be clear, include several stages to cater for the frequency and severity of the breach and be agreed to by all team members following their input. It is also important that at each team meeting someone takes the role of 'norm observer'.

A tap on the table

To see how this plays out, here's an example from one school we have worked with. Staff at the school decided to use a non-verbal cue as the first step to signify a norm was being broken during a meeting.

This was basically just a tap on the table to remind people that a norm was being broken.

That tap on the table can be taken as a non-verbal reminder, a little like: "Let's bring it back a bit" or "We're talking over each other". The tap acts as a reminder that someone's behaviour is impacting on the team's effectiveness.

The important part of this step in the breach process is that it's non-verbal. We don't want to stop the flow of the discussions and people's ideas at this point, but we do need to make everyone aware of and stop the behaviour impacting the team.

At this tap, everyone around the meeting table – not just the person who might be breaking the norm - suddenly thinks, "Oh, hang on, a norm's been broken". This will remind all team members to take stock and reflect on their behaviour, which is usually enough for everyone to consciously modify and regulate their behaviour before progressing with the discussion. It's important at this stage of the process that the person who is breaking the norm isn't identified. It's not about who, but about issuing a reminder to all that a norm is being broken.

In the highest functioning teams we have worked with, all team members have been given the authority to issue the tap, if they are concerned that a behaviour is impacting the team's effectiveness.

A more formal discussion

If a norm continues to be breached, then the next stage of the breach procedure is to table a more formal discussion on the next meeting agenda, framed by the question: "So what can we do to assist you/our team to ensure that this team expectation is being met?"

Basically, this step ensures that the team's collective power is harnessed in developing tangible strategies to overcome the issue. By holding a frank, open and honest discussion, the team goes into problem solving mode and continues to develop and build skills in the area that requires strengthening.

This step also reminds us that norms or their associated behaviours are not set in stone. A norm or behaviour descriptor doesn't have to stay in place for a whole year or even the whole term. If team members find that they've really elevated their capabilities to the point where a specific norm or behaviour descriptor becomes obsolete, the question arises: Do we need this team norm or behaviour as part of our team norms any longer?

In such a situation, the team may then consider whether it's time to think about a more relevant behaviour, and even devise a new norm that will allow the team to build to an even higher level of effectiveness.

As can be seen, this second step of the staged breach procedure involves tabling a more formal team discussion that takes a proactive and positive approach to support adherence to the norm, or associated behavioural expectations.

Gathering support from above

We all know it's extremely difficult to work with team members who don't feel that their needs in the change process have been met. Sometimes, because we're out of ideas, we need to gather additional ideas and strategies on how the team can help those people come on board. However, this is not a punitive thing where we browbeat the person into submission until they get it 'right'.

Rather, each stage in the breach procedure is about creating a culture of support and learning. We access as many people as possible to gather ideas, to elevate meetings to the point where behaviours that negatively impact on the team achieving its aims are eliminated. So, the third and final step of the norm breach procedure is to involve the school's senior leadership in the discussion of the norm breach.

It's important to emphasise that we would hope that team members themselves are able to handle and deal with any breaches of norms by coming up with solutions and strategies that overcome the undesirable behaviour. However, we recommend that teams do include this third step in the process, because if we truly believe that the work we're undertaking at the meeting is vital to the organisation's success, any continued and constant interruption can't be tolerated.

Indeed, if the work of the team is for some reason being interrupted repeatedly, then there has to be a process where support can be sought from the next level of leadership within the school to protect valuable disciplined collaborative outcomes.

Entering this more formal stage of the process can be difficult because it's not always easy to raise these issues with a colleague who doesn't appear to be complying. So it's important to have this stage as a clear step in the team's norm breach procedure. Again, it goes back to: "Why is this important?" We may need to remind ourselves and our colleagues that this is not personal. It's about the behaviour, which we've tried to overcome within the team, that's continuing to negatively impact on us being successful in the achievement of our collaborative endeavours.

At this stage, a more senior school leader might be asked to chair a discussion of the issue at a subsequent team meeting, with the goal of exploring further strategies that the team or individual might use to try to overcome the issue. Or it might be a more formal meeting between the team leader, a senior leader and the person having trouble complying with the norm. No matter what form the discussion takes, the focus is on addressing and overcoming the reasons that are contributing to the continued non-compliance.

Final considerations

It's becoming more and more common for teams to have norms. But creating norms and operationalising them are two very different things. If we've created norms through compliance or because "we've been told we must have them" but they are not actually lived, discussed or embedded into the team's practice, they're really not worth the paper they're written on.

Likewise, some schools or teams latch on to the idea that: "We need norms because they will solve the interpersonal issues we are having at our meetings". It's important that the creation of norms and the use of norms isn't seen as the end point in itself. Norms must serve the constant purpose of making sure each meeting is as effective and purposeful as it can be so that the team's collaborative outcomes are not jeopardised.

Here's something to consider as you ponder whether your team is using norms effectively. Is the level of effectiveness and purposefulness of the team the same, say, during the eighth meeting as it was during the first meeting? If it is the same, this is a clear indicator that the norms are not serving their purpose. The team should be getting increasingly efficient in the collaborative practices they use at meetings, because they have used norms as a way of deliberately identifying and developing the collaborative skills they can get better at.

This is where the team norm observer role becomes an essential component of the team's continuous improvement and development. As we will explore shortly, the norm observer should be engaging in the team's dialogue and the discussion, while also keeping an eye out for any behaviours that might be limiting or hindering the team's collaborative endeavours. After all, we're trying to enhance our collaborative endeavours and our collaborative dialogue.

However, keep in mind that the role of norm observers does not equate to being the "norm police", with their eyes focused on spotting every breach. Their role is about making sure meetings are purposeful and effective and identify areas the team can work on to make them even more so.

In Summary

When used optimally, team norms are a vital element for teams to leverage and master in team meetings that really matter. They improve the experience of participants at the meeting, the outcomes of the meeting and serve the beneficiaries of the work of the meeting.

Make sure everyone understands what norms are and their purpose

It doesn't really matter what norms are called. But all team members must understand that norms articulate the behaviours they have all agreed to honour, in order to make the meeting as effective and purposeful as possible. Each team member needs to know that norms are the professional, collective behavioural commitments they make to get the best out of each other. And that such norms reduce the risk of personal conflicts arising or escalating, making it easier to achieve the meeting's intended outcomes. Norms make the meeting a safe space for the people to do the work.

As a starting point to developing your norms, review which current behaviours are impeding the team's productivity

If you've already had some meetings and there's a feeling they haven't been effective or productive, dissect the situation and ask: "What behaviours might have contributed to this?" Make sure you don't point the finger at individual team members. Instead, be very careful and intentional about pinpointing the behaviours that appear to have negatively impacted the productivity of meetings. Pose the question: "What behaviours could we commit to which would ensure these situations don't arise in the future?"

Base norm conversations on the team's purpose

Frame these discussions around the team's broad purpose in meeting, such as:

- Why does our team exist?
- What do we expect to achieve together?
- Who do we need to be, both individually and collectively, to achieve our purposes and ensure that what we do and who we are achieve outcomes that 'matter'?

Remember that it's not about personal preference or what a particular person may want. It's about who our team needs to be to ensure we are successful at each meeting.

Framing the discussion in this way ensures the norms are created, lived and breathed, which in turn supports and enhances the work of the team.

Design a breach process that's easy to understand and implement

This breach procedure must be a multi-stage process that each team member takes ownership of and commits to. Each person must realise the importance of having an agreed breach procedure, and appreciate how the process supports them to be the person they need to be at the meeting - so that the collaborative outcomes of the team are realised.

Ultimately, when used well, team norms are a vital tool to leverage in developing mastery of team meetings that really matter.

Taking stock:

Where is your team in relation to this essential?

Rate your team's current performance level using the following scale:

1 We're unaware of this
2 We are aware of this, but it is not yet evident in our team's practices
3 We are fully conscious of applying this
4 Automaticity – we automatically apply it in our team practice and functioning

We have clearly defined and articulated team norms.

1	2	3	4

We include the team norms on the agenda of each meeting.

1	2	3	4

We have a focus norm for each team meeting.

1	2	3	4

We use our norm breach procedure when there is a breach.

1	2	3	4

We review our team norms at the end of each meeting, in terms of how well our team is going and how well the norms are supporting the team's purposes.

1	2	3	4

How are you facilitating this action?

What might you need to stop doing, continue doing or start doing?

How does your team need to *show up* to increase impact, and what might this mean for you as facilitator?

2.
Get clear

Ensure all team members are clear about their role

In our observations of teams over the past 30 years, we've noticed that when team members aren't clear about their roles, it negatively impacts the team's effectiveness.

Conversely, when team members are very clear about their roles and what is required of them – including what they need to do (the work) and who they need to be – then their meetings are more likely to 'matter'.

A team working collaboratively should have the following roles:

- Chairperson
- Facilitator
- Minute taker
- Norm observer

While there are several ways in which the roles can be described, we suggest the following:

Chairperson –

Many teams in schools have a team leader who has a hierarchical position in relation to their role outside the team meeting. This person may act as the chairperson of the meeting. This role involves making sure that the team meeting schedule and agenda for each meeting is communicated to all team members. The chairperson may also follow up any implementation issues regarding decisions/actions made at the meeting. At the meeting they may also act as the meeting facilitator, although this doesn't always have to be the case.

Facilitator –

Facilitates the team's processes during the meeting. The facilitator ensures the team achieves its aims and attends to agenda items within the determined time frame. The team facilitator oversees the implementation and adherence to the protocol the team uses as they address each agenda item.

Minute taker –

Documents the meeting by making a written record. Teams need to decide if they wish the minutes to include all contributions to dialogue and discussion, just the decisions made, or follow up to be undertaken by all (or specified) team members. Minute takers also check with team members where needed to make sure the documentation is accurate.

Norm observer –

Observes whether behaviours exhibited in the meeting align with the team's agreed behaviour norms.

The names of the team members allocated to each role should be clearly listed on the meeting agenda.

To combine or not to combine roles?

As mentioned above, for some kinds of collaborative team meetings, the chairperson and the facilitator are combined within the same role. This is particularly true of the process we outline for collaborative teams in a PLC in our book, *Collaborative Teams That Work* (Sloper & Grift, 2020). In these types of collaborative teams, where the roles are also rotated, the chair/facilitator may or may not be the official leader of the group. To illustrate what we mean here, in a PLC which comprises English teachers at a school, the head of department or faculty coordinator may not necessarily always take on the role of the chairperson/facilitator if that PLC has a practice of rotating roles.

In other types of school teams, such as a senior leadership team, the team may decide they want to nominate a chair for the overall meeting – but also sometimes appoint separate facilitators for agenda items.

Ultimately, it is up to the school and/or a school's various teams to determine whether they wish to combine the role of chairperson and facilitator in one, or if they wish to keep these roles distinct. Whatever the decision and subsequent practice, it is still paramount that all members of that team are very clear on what that role requires of them. This not only relates to the work they need to do, but also to who their team needs them to be to successfully lead the meeting, or pursue the agenda item in a way to ensure that both the processes and the outcomes 'matter'.

Importance of role allocation and timing

Team roles should be briefly revisited and reviewed at the end of each meeting, then allocated for the next meeting. For example, you might take a quick moment to discuss and decide who is taking on each role at the next meeting. Will it be the same person, or will roles be rotated?

This gives the nominated chairperson/facilitator the chance to liaise with the team leader ahead of time, to ensure they understand the topics and the agenda items and undertake any necessary research or preparation to make the next meeting as effective as possible.

Teams also need to ensure these roles are allocated and operationalised because team members' ability to fulfil these roles will develop over time, and with experience in the role. As this development occurs, the effectiveness of team meetings, along with the team's collective efficacy and capacity to achieve the organisation's goals, are enhanced.

A chairperson/facilitator can measure his or her success by reviewing how well the team was able to achieve the objectives of the meeting and evaluate the success of the processes implemented in the meeting. They can also evaluate how well the team adhered to the agreed-on team norms to make these things happen.

Getting clear around the 'role' of the positional team leader

It might be that as a new team is formed, the 'nominated' team leader with positional power (such as head of department/faculty coordinator/team leader etc) feels more comfortable taking on the chairperson or facilitation role. They might think this is wise because they can model what the role entails, and build the capabilities of other team members in understanding how successful collaboration is activated through skilful facilitation.

Indeed, often the very title of 'team leader' implies that this is the person who's going to be making all the decisions. But to build a true spirit of collaboration and ensure all voices are heard, it is important that the team leader's status and influence at the meeting is seen to be on an equal footing with all other team members. At a team meeting that matters to everyone, the voice of the team leader shouldn't have any more sway than anyone else's.

If the role of team leader is a nominated responsibility in a school's leadership structure, it's important that the role this person assumes at the meeting is clarified and clear to all. We are strong advocates for, and see higher levels of collaboration being achieved, when the nominated team leader can drop the title of team leader at the meeting and operate collaboratively as a facilitator of process, rather than the arbitrator of all decisions. This is even more actively demonstrated when the team leader can empower others to assume this role at team meetings.

Why it makes sense to rotate roles

We believe that it's a really good idea to rotate or share the role of chair.

If the team is truly committed to achieving its purpose and advancing the mission of the school, there are great benefits in having team discussions that have a clearly identified, but rotating facilitator. Relational trust is enhanced when all team members feel valued by being given the opportunity to lead these meetings.

Role rotation has many benefits for teams. Role rotation can contribute to the effectiveness of meetings as each team member develops and grows their capacity to contribute to the team's purposes. At the same time, this positively impacts the organisation's purposes and mission, and ultimately helps the entire team become more successful.

It can also help to develop the team's collective efficacy – the team's belief in its capacity to make a difference and achieve its outcomes. This then increases the team's impact, its capacity to make a difference, and the ability to do work that 'matters' to those for whom it 'matters'. By trusting in an individual's potential to develop, we enable them to make a greater contribution to the team's goals and purposes, which in turn increases their commitment to the team and its goals. It also potentially leads to a higher sense of self and professional worth for the individual.

Providing opportunities to grow and contribute through rotating roles also sends a signal that each team member is valued, and has the capacity to contribute and do meaningful work that matters for the team and those they serve. This enhances job satisfaction and can lead to greater discretionary effort on the part of team members. They feel trusted, valued, and welcome to fully participate. They feel like their team leader is truly committed to the learning and thriving of all the team members. There is a sense of authenticity and congruence.

It is possible to be even more democratic in school team meetings of a more general nature by further subdivision of the roles, whereby the chairperson does not facilitate every item on the agenda unless it is something for which they have 'ownership' or expertise. The effectiveness of leadership team meetings can also be increased by allocating responsibility for running the agenda items to the team member who has ownership or authority over the particular matter as part of their role. That person may have proposed the item or been allocated to it.

In this case, the chairperson would be required to liaise with the 'owner' of an agenda item, who would communicate with the group about the purpose of that item, the preparation needed by team members, and the processes to be used. This process further builds the capacity of all team members. However, a word of caution: it is important that the 'facilitator' of the agenda item does not push their own agenda – and that the purpose and processes and products of the agenda item are clearly linked to the team's agreed work that matters, for example linking it to school or team goals. Indeed, sometimes it can be more effective to ensure that a more 'neutral' team member facilitates the exploration and processes of an agenda item, particularly an item that sparks heightened emotions, strong competing interests or has a history of tension.

Why the minute taker needs to contribute to the meeting, too

Obviously, we're all familiar with minute taking, and every school keeps records or minutes on what goes on in meetings.

But when it comes to an effective meeting, we believe the minute taker should only record the main decisions made by the team, in a way that accurately summarises what everyone agreed to.

In an effective and productive meeting, the minute taker does not need to record every point of the discussion that's led to the ultimate decision. We don't want the minute taker to be so busy writing minutes that they can't contribute to the meeting. We've observed many meetings where there's a dedicated minute taker who finds the role so onerous that it literally takes them out of the meeting and robs the team of their input. They become so immersed in the role and recording the minutes that their voice becomes lost or is non-existent.

Instead, the designated minute taker should be absorbing, listening, and contributing on an equal footing with all other team members. Then, as the team gets closer to deciding or needing to reach a consensus, the minute taker should record accurately what the team decision is and what follow-up is required (by who and when).

The role of norm observer

Another role is that of norm observer - someone who has the responsibility of formally monitoring and reporting on the team's use of designated team norms.

This person can have a huge impact on the success of a meeting. They are really asking or reminding the team: who do we need to be at the meeting to be effective in what we're trying to achieve, and ensure we accomplish what matters?

As examined previously, the actual norms that guide the behaviour of team members obviously need to be meaningful and relevant to each team, but you do need a norm observer to keep an eye on team members' adherence to the norms. They must report their observations to the team at the meeting's conclusion, so that team members' ability to work effectively together can be continually strengthened and enhanced. This also consolidates the fact that it's not just about the learning and growth of the team, but individuals too.

It is also very helpful when individual team members reflect on their own adherence – not just the team's – to the focus norm that has been agreed on. This ensures that team members pay conscious attention to getting better at adhering to and using norms to support processes.

The goal of each meeting should be not only to 'get the work' done, but also get better and better at getting this work done. This is an important part of continuous improvement, which can be helped by having a person nominated to the norm observer role at each meeting. This ultimately shows that how we are being with each other as we do the work matters just as much as the work we do together. By dedicating time to this process, it shows we value it, which also signals that we truly do want all team members to be able to participate wholeheartedly. It shows that the norms 'matter' and should be committed to – not just formed as 'lip service' to some decree from above.

Keeping track of time

The last role we'll discuss here is that of the meeting timekeeper.

This might seem obvious, but you'd be surprised at how many times we've seen time get away at meetings because this role hasn't been carried out well or doesn't exist at all.

The meeting timekeeper monitors and communicates to team members the time used during the meeting dialogue and discussion on the various items on the meeting agenda.

We use both the words dialogue and discussion deliberately here because we believe each play a different role in a meeting, depending on the nature of the agenda item. Jason Combs (2019) describes **dialogue** as "a communicative process in which people with different perspectives seek understanding".

On the other hand, Oxford Languages define **discussion** as "the action or process of talking about something in order to reach a decision or to exchange idea". We make this distinction throughout this handbook and encourage teams to think about the kind of talk they are engaged in. Does the agenda item require a search for collective understanding through exploring each other's thinking (dialogue) or an exchange of ideas in order to reach consensus or a decision (discussion)?

Depending on the nature of the agenda item, time at any meeting might be used to build shared understanding - and other times dedicated to deciding. This time should not be left to chance; it needs to be allocated and adhered to.

For example, how long should team members spend seeking to understand a problem? And how long does your team need to make a decision, or decide on which action they need to take?

Consideration of these questions allows the team to allocate the required time to each agenda item, based on the nature of the conversation needed. This subsequently provides the time-keeper with a reference point for their monitoring.

A sidenote on timekeeping

Recently, we were working with a school, observing their teams, and noticed they'd become efficient in the way their timekeeper role had evolved.

Originally, their timekeeper was efficacious, wanting to move through agenda items at great pace. But over a period, the team had learned the role of the timekeeper was to also give gentle reminders along the lines of: "Everyone, we've got three minutes left on this item. Do we think we're going to reach agreement within these three minutes? Or might we need to extend this item?"

In an effective meeting, the timekeeper's role is not to abruptly curtail discussions and dialogue, but to ensure the team is aware of how much time is remaining for each agenda item. This way, team members become more efficient in their conversations.

In Summary

All teams require members to have specific roles, irrespective of the size of the team

- Even in a team of two or three, make sure each member has a role so that meetings become increasingly effective and productive
- In a small team, sometimes each team member might have more than one role
- You might think "but we know each other really well" or "our meetings run well the way they are, and we don't need specific roles". However, the point is to continually enhance professional discussion and dialogue, and to become as

increasingly productive as you can to ensure meeting objectives are achieved and that outcomes and processes matter.

Ensure everyone's clear on their role

- Make sure everyone is crystal clear on their role (and what the role entails) before the meeting, so there's no allocating tasks on the hop and wasting precious time at the start of the meeting.
- Having clearly understood meeting roles allows each member to get straight on to the important work they need to undertake at that meeting.

Build team members' capabilities to fill a variety of roles

- Meetings should become a source of professional learning, as you support one another to get better at each role, have discussions about how to enhance the impact of the roles and, if needed, carry out research into that role.
- By building the capability of each team member, meetings become more effective, which ultimates benefits student learning.
- It pays to focus not only on the work that needs to be done in meetings, but on building the capabilities of team members to do the work.

There may be additional roles that a team comes up with. Any new role should focus on enhancing the productivity and impact of the team. For example, some teams have added the role of 'process observer'. This person's role is to observe how effectively the team adopts and participates in certain processes at a meeting, to achieve the desired purposes. The 'process observer' would then reflect this back to the team at the end of a meeting.

Taking stock:

Where is your team in relation to this essential?

Rate your team's current performance level using the following scale:

1 We're unaware of this
2 We are aware of this, but it is not yet evident in our team's practices
3 We are fully conscious of applying this
4 Automaticity - we automatically apply it in our team practice and functioning

Our team has clarity around team roles.

1	2	3	4

We allocate roles for the next meeting at the conclusion of each meeting.

1	2	3	4

We reflect on how effectively the roles are supporting the team's work.

1	2	3	4

How are you facilitating this action?

What might you need to stop doing, continue doing or start doing?

How does your team need to show up to increase impact and what might this mean for you as facilitator?

3.

Make it Relevant

Ensure agenda items progress the team's purpose or goals

When we consider agendas of team meetings that really matter, we propose that regardless of the type of meetings, they must all address the 3 Ps of great meetings: Purpose, People and Process. It's only by doing this that we ensure we maximise the impact of the work we do in the team meeting, both in terms of the way we do it, and how our people feel as a result of their participation.

Purpose

Are we really clear on the reason why we are meeting, and are we clearly articulating that to our people before they arrive?

And while they are at the meeting, are we making connections between what we are doing and how it helps us meet our purpose?

Do we check in with our people at the start of our meeting and provide opportunities to seek clarification on why we are meeting, and anything else they may be wondering about?

The articulation of our purpose also needs to include a clear idea of the product of the meeting - that is the outcomes of the meeting in relation to our purpose. Are we clear on what we hope to achieve?

There always needs to be something tangible that our participants walk away with, whether that's increased knowledge, or greater understanding or skills. This purpose always needs to be articulated in a way that includes the outcomes that will be enjoyed.

People

Are we clear on who needs to be there and why?

Have we communicated this in a timely manner, so these team members are 'primed' and motivated to participate wholeheartedly?

Have we made clear what is expected of them in terms of their participation?

Process

Are we clear on what processes and protocols we will use to achieve our purpose and product?

And have we let our people know what preparation they might need to do prior to the team meeting to be able to contribute?

Do these processes suit the purpose of the meeting; are they valid processes to use to achieve our outcomes?

Have we communicated with our participants about the processes we plan to use?

In our work with schools, there are two broad types of school teams - teams that work collaboratively, and teams that implement a collaborative process. Let's really get clear on this distinction to ensure that we are not adding to the confusion we often see in schools.

As mentioned above, year level teams, pastoral care teams, vertical teams or faculty/discipline-based/curriculum teams might be formed to work collaboratively on achieving a goal or completing tasks by working collaboratively. We believe the strongest teams are those that form to implement a collaborative process. This should focus solely on carrying out action research through the implementation of cycles of learning, to improve the individual and collective teaching practice of team members. We refer to such teams in our book *Collaborative Teams That Work* (Sloper & Grift, 2020), as collaborative teams (in a PLC) and believe there are two different inquiry cycles that could be implemented by such teams, depending on how the teams have been formed.

The three Ps of meetings apply to the planning of any meeting agenda for any school team. However let's take a more in-depth look at how to ensure agenda items are progressing the process of action research, to investigate and improve the teaching practice of team members.

Agenda items that progress the collaborative team's progress in the PLC process of action research and implementation of the cycle of learning process

Over time, as collaborative teams increase their understanding of the true focus of their collaborative endeavours, and as school structures are modified and strengthened to allow this focus at team meetings, the alignment of the tasks focused on at meetings and the stages of action research become stronger.

Your team might not yet be at this stage, which is fine, or it might not be applicable depending on the purpose of the meeting. But hopefully over time, you can ensure agenda items progress the team's action research and implementation of the cycle of learning process. That's particularly the case if the team has a genuine desire to improve student learning, by focusing its collaborative endeavours on truly transforming and improving the impact of teaching practice.

In our book *Collaborative Teams That Work* (Sloper & Grift, 2020), we include a sample meeting agenda. This includes diagrams of the typical phases in the two different cycles of learning, as a visual reminder of the process teams are engaged in.

The first cycle details the typical actions for a team that has been formed on the basis that they're delivering the same content to their students. During this kind of team meeting, the main agenda items will be discussing the content they're going to deliver, teaching methodologies and the assessments they're using to monitor the learning of their students and the impact of their teaching practice. Such teams are usually made up of team members teaching the same year level or curriculum area.

The first cycle of learning extends the PLC at Work® research and is driven by the four critical PLC questions which underpin the team's action research. The actual agenda items that form each meeting agenda arise as a natural consequence as these teams address these questions:

1. What do we want students to learn?
2. How will we know are students are learning?
3. How will we respond when some students don't learn?
4. How will we extend the learning of students who are already proficient?

(Dufour et al. 2019 pp 8-9)

These questions might not be as relevant for a team whose members do not deliver the same content. This is where the actions of the alternative cycle of learning might be more appropriate.

The second cycle of learning diagram outlines the main actions that a team formed to investigate an inquiry question together might undertake. This cycle of learning is more suited to teams of educators coming together regularly, who don't necessarily teach the same content but are going to inquire into a learning issue they're striving to collectively overcome.

We have seen this second approach work well in secondary schools where a group of teachers form a team, or in a primary school where specialist teachers form a team. Members were not necessarily all teaching the same content area, but were investigating how they could collaboratively overcome a common learning issue they were all focusing on in their classrooms. In this case their investigation was more appropriately underpinned by these five questions:

1. What student learning issue are we seeking to address?
2. How will we know we have addressed the student learning issue?
3. How might we overcome the issue?
4. What actions will we trial?
5. Which actions will we now adopt to enrich our instructional practice?

As with the previously described cycle of learning, *Collaborative Teams That Work* (Sloper & Grift, 2020) the agenda items for each meeting arise as a natural consequence of these teams addressing these questions.

Are team members clear that the process they use is dictated by how the team was formed, and the goal the team is trying to achieve?

Meetings are much more effective, productive, and focused when team members understand the process that guides the work that they are doing at the meeting. We would argue that in a team implementing a collaborative process, team members must have a common inquiry (i.e. focus of their action research) they are investigating and trying to overcome together. This demands discussion and dialogue to reach a conclusion that enhances their teaching practice. If a team is not formed on this basis, they can work on collaborative tasks together, but the fruits of this collaboration may not have the same impact.

This does not negate other school teams which form to complete collaborative tasks together; these are still important teams and often contribute to moving school's closer to the achievement of their mission. However, we see such teams as secondary to collaborative teams in a PLC which are more impactful in achieving the fundamental mission of all schools - high levels of learning for all students. Teams formed to undertake collaborative tasks should be seen as a support to collaborative teams implementing the collaborative process.

What's your sense of the teams that meet in your school? How might team members respond to the following questions:

- Why does our meeting exist?
- What's the reason for working together, and is this supported by the items included on the agenda?

Agenda items need to support the purpose of the meeting

Any item that is included in the agenda should support the broad purpose or purposes of the team's actual existence - its reason for being. Often 'stray' items, or items unrelated to the core purpose of the team, may be added into the agenda when team members are not clear of the team's overall purpose. While such an item might promote much discussion, the discussion will likely not result in any tangible action being taken by the team. However, when an item is directly related to the team's purpose, members will feel a much greater sense of satisfaction and achievement. That's because they can see how it will contribute to the outcomes the team is trying to achieve, and the difference they are wanting to make.

So, make sure that your team has a very clear and shared understanding of its core purpose in meetings. Make sure your team knows if the expectation is for it to complete tasks collaboratively or to implement a collaborative process. There is a big difference. Clarity around purpose (and therefore process) requires regular open conversations about how the team's work is contributing to which part of the school's vision/mission or strategic plan. When these connections are clearly communicated, teachers are more likely to be feel purposeful, connected and motivated, as they can see how their combined efforts contribute to the school's overall vision for improvement.

A practical example for a team that is implementing the collaborative process

Here's a practical example to help make it clearer.

A collaborative team in a PLC decides to use a meeting to review the learning data from a quick check assessment they've done. They have been teaching a unit of work and want to get some information back by including the following two agenda items:

a) How their students are going
b) How impactful their teaching practice has been.

These agenda items directly relate to the purpose for this team coming together. This team was formed because they are the English teachers in a secondary school. The team had been focusing on improving their teaching of more complex and interesting sentence construction to their students. After teaching the skills and concepts for several weeks, they had decided they needed to check on the impact of their teaching.

Knowing that the analysis of the quick check data wouldn't take the whole meeting, they also decided they would start to brainstorm the key skills and knowledge they wanted students to learn in their upcoming focus on punctuation. To do this, the team decided to collaboratively map the learning pathway for each of their year levels. If time permitted at the meeting, they also committed to developing some quick checks assessments for any students who were struggling with some of these essential punctuation skills.

As you can see, the two agenda items for this team's upcoming meeting directly supported the purpose of the team, and involved the team inquiring into the best teaching practices to ensure all students reach proficiency in the identified skills. Any suggestions that didn't advance or support the team's inquiry through action research were rejected and not included in the proposed agenda.

Questions of inquiry

As advanced above, the most effective collaborative teams are those formed based on implementing an inquiry into an aspect of their teaching practice, or a learning issue. This belief has implications for the way items are stated on the agenda. Just including a heading in the agenda – for example, 'Review the learning data' – is not going to be enough for a team truly implementing the collaborative process!

Our experience working with highly effective collaborative teams convincingly suggests that it's more helpful to the team and the work they will do to frame such a heading as a question of inquiry. In this case the question the team might potentially explore is: 'What is this data telling us about the learning of our students and the strength of our teaching practice?'

The team may have also determined that the best protocol for analysing this type of data is the 'What? So What? Now What?' protocol, which they had previously used successfully. This would also be listed on the agenda, along with the timeframe allocated for the discussion.

So, on their agenda this item would appear as follows:

Agenda Item:
Review the learning data

'What is this data telling us about the learning of our students and the strength of our teaching practice?'
Protocol to be used: "What? So What? Now What?
Time allocated: 20 minutes

By framing the agenda item as an inquiry question, the team is opening up the range of ideas and possibilities, rather than narrowing the scope of their investigation. These inquiry questions support the team by ensuring they are only considering tasks that underpin the stages of action research.

Outlining the protocol that will be used for each specific agenda item is also a great example of how to build the capacity of team members to fulfil and enact the roles we outlined earlier. For example, the chairperson/facilitator of the meeting is strengthening their capacity to render the path easier for the team by confidently implementing the 'What? So What? Now What?' protocol in a considered fashion. The chairperson can also continue to build his/her capabilities to have team members reach consensus, as the item is addressed.

While our focus here has been on the practice of framing agenda items as inquiry questions for collaborative teams in a PLC, we also advocate this practice for all team meetings, for all kinds of teams in schools.

Administrative items

As mentioned above, an essential attribute of a successful and highly productive collaborative team implementing the collaborative process is its ability to filter agenda items through the lens of the team's purpose. We know from experience, however, that it is not always possible to filter out all items that are not strictly related to advancing the 'right work' of the collaborative team meeting. The meeting forum provides a convenient and often irresistible way of communicating with or gathering input from staff, while they are together. on a wide variety of school issues and topics. This is also true for teams completing tasks collaboratively.

Recognising this, we suggest on our sample agenda that you might allocate a spot for such administrative items that can't be avoided. We refer to such items as 'admin items'. As emphasised above, these items are the ones that, over time, your team will hopefully learn to minimise, or at least handle expediently. We acknowledge that these items might be important to someone, but they shouldn't be allocated the same amount of precious meeting time as other items on the agenda that relate to the team's core purpose.

The structuring of the sample agenda is deliberate in making team members aware of which items they should be focusing the most time and attention on. On the flipside, by having an allocated space on the agenda, it highlights that quicker admin items don't need to take up too much valuable meeting time.

This is also important to appreciate if you're part of a school's leadership or executive hierarchy. Experience has taught us that these 'admin items' are often imposed on the team's agenda by the school's leadership. So it's important that school leaders don't accidentally sabotage their team's endeavours by imposing items or requirements that distract teams from their core business.

A lack of focus

Take this practical example. We recently worked with a group of principals and assistant principals from a range of schools. It became clear a common concern was why many teams implementing the collaborative process at their various schools couldn't focus their meetings on tasks that specifically related to improving teaching practice by implementing the cycle of learning process to move them close to achieving higher levels of learning for all students.

When we reviewed a selection of team agendas, we quickly noticed an imbalance between agenda items listed under the 'learning' section and the 'admin' section. In many cases the admin items outnumbered learning focused items four to one. This uneven spread was clearly robbing many teams of the time they really needed to spend focusing on their real purpose – improving teaching practice and thus ultimately improving student learning.

Check the team's agenda items require the whole team to engage in collaborative dialogue and discussion

For teams to produce outcomes that really 'matter', we need to ensure agenda items do require all team members to engage in collaborative dialogue and discussion. Many times, we've seen agenda items included (we've at times been guilty of this ourselves as both contributors and leaders) that waste the valuable time of some team members, because they are not affected by that particular item. One of the rarest commodities in schools is time and even rarer, the time for teams to meet. With time being so scarce, it is vital that items included in the team agenda engage and impact all team members, not only in the work they must do, but also in terms of their impact on their sense of identity and intrinsic purpose. Of course, this is tied closely to the reason the team members have been placed in the team together in the first place.

Checking that the team is spending time on things that matter is initially part of the team leader's role, and then becomes each team member's role as they propose and review what items are going to be included in the agenda.

In Summary

Understand the primary purpose of the meeting

For teams completing tasks collaboratively and teams implementing the collaborative process, understanding the purpose of the meeting is vital as it can act as a filter as to what should, and what actually ends up on the agenda. Agenda items should clearly align with the team's purpose. And items that don't should be rejected or, at the very least, minimised.

Check the team's agenda items require participation of the whole team

Make sure agenda items are relevant to all team members so we do not waste their valuable time. Such experiences create frustration and irritation in team members and can damage your credibility as a facilitator or team leader.

Know thy process

All team members need to clearly understand the process they will be following at their meeting. If it's a team that's been formed based on the common content they deliver, or the common inquiry into a learning issue they are investigating, the process should be one of action research.

In our book *Collaborative Teams That Work* (Sloper & Grift, 2020) we clearly outline the actions and tasks collaborative teams work through as they implement action research and the cycles of learning process. These actions and tasks inform the agenda items, thus providing a useful resource for these types of collaborative teams.

Think about how you record your agenda items

The biggest complaint we repeatedly hear from schools is that they don't have enough time. We know it's impossible to create more time, so it's important we make the precious time we have for meeting with our colleagues as productive as possible. One way of doing this is to frame our agenda items as inquiry questions. That's because these questions require team members to engage in dialogue and discussion and call on the collective expertise of all team members as they try to answer the questions. While our focus here has primarily been on the practice of framing agenda items as inquiry questions for collaborative teams in a PLC, we also advocate this practice for any kind of team meetings within schools. The same benefits will follow.

And remember, if the suggested item can't be framed in this way, ask yourself: "Why are we putting it on the agenda?"

Taking stock:

Where is your team in relation to this essential?

Rate your team's current performance level using the following scale:

1 We're unaware of this
2 We are aware of this, but it is not yet evident in our team's practices
3 We are fully conscious of applying this
4 Automaticity – we automatically apply it in our team practice and functioning

Our team understands our primary purpose in meeting.

1	2	3	4

We ensure that our agenda items are relevant to all team members.

1	2	3	4

We prioritise agenda items that relate to our core purpose over admin items.

1	2	3	4

We clearly communicate the processes and protocols to be used for the exploration of each agenda item.

1	2	3	4

We communicate any preparation required in a timely manner.

1	2	3	4

How are you facilitating this action?

What might you need to stop doing, continue doing or start doing?

How does your team need to show up to increase impact and what might this mean for you as facilitator?

Build your Skills

Continue to strengthen meeting facilitation skills as we work through the agenda

I f you are committed to developing mastery in conducting team meetings that really matter, each team meeting can be seen as an opportunity for the meeting chairperson or the team meeting facilitator to practise and strengthen their facilitation skills. It's all about developing mastery in this important role.

The planning and facilitation of each agenda item provides the opportunity to develop and strengthen our skills of facilitation and, most importantly, raise our level of self-awareness regarding the role, which allows us to continue to get better at it. And by continuing to get better at facilitating, we make sure we're supporting our team to make meetings matter even more!

In addition to the work to be undertaken collaboratively, we need to pay attention to how we will deliberately foster the commitment and engagement of our team members in the work, so that it is rewarding and satisfying for them. To do so requires consideration of several matters.

As the facilitator, think about how you want your team to feel during the meeting. Then think about how you will achieve that. For example, what might your team need of you if you want them to leave feeling satisfied and energised?

Here is a list of questions to consider:

- What will you need to focus on in yourself in terms of your tone of voice, stance, posture, or positioning of yourself in relation to the group?
- How will you help your team members transition from the current concerns of their day to the collaborative work at hand?
- How will you organise the furniture in the room to ensure it encourages the kinds of collaborative tasks you have planned on the agenda?
- What kinds of tasks and protocols are you planning, and will they achieve your purpose - both in terms of the work to be done and how you want your team members to feel?
- Is there a balance of different kinds of tasks and activities?
- Are short rest breaks built in for team members to stretch or move around?
- Are refreshments available so that team members are catered for and don't feel hungry, particularly if the meeting takes place at the end of the day?
- How will you build and foster a sense of caring and community within the team?

Indeed, consider what values you might need to hold true to if being a facilitator is truly your identity. What kinds of capabilities and skills might you need to ensure you possess or commit to developing? What actions and behaviours might you need to exhibit that are consistent with your identity as a facilitator? How will that allow you to resonate with authenticity as a result of the congruence in what you think, do and say?

And how might you arrange your environment and yourself in terms of the physical configurations of furniture and where you position yourself in the room?

We have some very practical tips to offer to help you operationalise an agenda in a more powerful way and consider it through the lens of facilitation and developing mastery over this important role.

The role of the facilitator

As mentioned above, the meeting chairperson role, (again, often referred to as the meeting facilitator), manages processes so that a team can plan, problem solve, share information, evaluate, and make decisions efficiently and effectively. The person performing this role at the meeting should also focus on improving team members' capacity to work together, and continually seek to improve the processes used at the meetings.

When a person is leading a meeting, it often involves improvisation. The facilitator needs to have the necessary knowledge and skills, as well as a clear sense of purpose, to make decisions on the spot while team members are interacting. A skilled facilitator is capable of attending to multiple things at once, like a juggler, and knows what to do even when faced with uncertainty (Garmston & Wellman, 2013). This requires being self-aware and self-regulating in the moment, as well as being 'team-aware'. You need to be able to reflect in the moment, to determine what's best to serve the team's desired purpose as it responds to each agenda item, while also ensuring team members feel valued, seen and heard.

Being a successful team facilitator is obviously quite a complex role and one that is vital to the success of the meeting, so it makes sense that the official, or designated team leader, might take on the facilitation role in the early stages of a team forming so that other team members are able to build their understanding of what the role truly is, as well as who we need to be as a facilitator.

Being conscious of our identity as a 'facilitator' which according to its Latin roots, means to 'make easier' or to 'render less difficult', is vital for success in this role. To master this role and identity requires us to choose both verbal and non-verbal behaviours that are congruent with this role and its associated identity. For a facilitator to truly make the collaborative team meeting's work and processes easier, they need to make conscious choices about things that will meet the emotional, psychological, physical, social and cognitive needs of participants, in order to achieve the meeting's purpose. This leads to greater authenticity and impact - leading to outcomes and feelings that matter.

Ultimately, effective facilitation requires more than telling team members what to do or think. In many ways, facilitation can also be seen as surrendering the power and influence that the title of team leader brings, and being able to take a neutral stance to allow the will of the team and true team collaboration to surface.

Note: you don't have to be showy to be a good facilitator, but you do need to be earnest in your commitment to creating clarity for all, to increasing levels of awareness for both self and team and to working at your facilitation skills to build confidence and trustworthy professional behaviours.

Particularly in a collaborative team in a PLC, we know that middle leadership is an absolute catalyst to improving student learning and teacher learning in schools, and the role of meeting facilitator often falls on the shoulders of middle leaders.

Here are some things that might be worth remembering when you take on this important role.

Three strategies to help you in the art of facilitating

Here are three strategies that can really help you juggle, and eventually develop, mastery over the many facets of the facilitator role. These strategies are adapted from the being purposeful strategies outlined in Five Ways of Being (Danvers, De Blasio & Grift, 2020) and The Adaptive School (Garmston & Wellman, 2013).

Honour and Divert

At a meeting, the facilitator might notice that when one team member speaks, several other team members appear annoyed, perhaps even rolling their eyes or looking repeatedly and intently at their watches, particularly in teams where norms haven't been internalised by team members. It's obvious, especially considering that non-verbal communication makes up a large amount of all communication to our colleagues, that the team member who is speaking is either consciously or unconsciously trying to dominate the discussion.

A skilful facilitator takes considered action to address this issue. The third time that this team member asks to contribute at the meeting, the facilitator does not call on them. Instead, they call on another team member or just close the discussion. This prevents the same behaviour being repeated. Later in the meeting, the facilitator tries to rehabilitate the team member's status by calling positive attention to a contribution they have made.

What this response emphasises is that the offending team member is a valued team member who can make valuable contributions, but it's important for the success of the team that all team members have the opportunity to make contributions to the discussion.

Some other alternatives to such a scenario that a facilitator might consider, depending on the context of the meeting, may be moving to another part of the room and asking if anyone in that area would like to contribute. For example, "Would anyone here like to add something?" This can be particularly effective if you're running a meeting that involves the whole staff, or a larger group of people. Moving to another area subtly signals that you are seeking another person to respond and avoids one person trying to dominate or take over the meeting, for whatever reason.

Always remember that the facilitator's relationship is with the team, not just the individual. It's the facilitator's role to develop the skills to strengthen the team's collaborative culture, which allows the team to continually move closer to realising its primary purpose.

Significance review

This strategy is particularly useful when team members are going off topic and the ensuing conversation may be of little or no relevance to the agenda item being dealt with. It is important to recognise this is not necessarily a deliberate act of disruption. It may be due to someone's personality type, for example, if someone is a little too excitable and starts going off on a tangent, or is not being self-reflective and noticing that their comments are not relevant to the agenda item being dealt with.

When using the significance review strategy, for a team member who says something that seems unrelated to the topic, the facilitator may question this in an approachable and curious way. They might, for example ask: "Colin, it might help us to understand how your comments relate to the topic being explored. I'm interested. I'm just trying to find the significance of what you have said to what we are discussing."

Obviously, that's very different than saying: "Colin, how is this of relevance to the topic being explored?" In this question, it's clear the facilitator thinks there's no relevance or significance, so it's always important to watch your wording.

You will notice in the first response that we invite the team member to explain the alignment between their words and the agenda item, under the positive assumption that there may be some. For some team members this might be helpful because they may have some connection in mind, and we're flagging the fact that we're just not fully understanding it. If the speaker can explain the significance, the conversation can proceed, and they can feel understood and valued because the facilitator has taken the time to make meaning and try to help the team member make a contribution to the team's work. And obviously if that's not the case, we take it off the table, redirect and move on.

A possible variation is for the facilitator to record the comment in some way (for example, on chart paper, in the meeting minutes, etc.) whilst making the comment, "So, Gavin, that's an interesting point. I'll note that down." This approach conveys to the person and the team, that while "this is not something we can look at now, we don't have time at this meeting and we're not going to allow time at this meeting to be sacrificed because of it", we are still interested in hearing about the idea later. Following this, the facilitator might, for example, decide to add the item to the next meeting's agenda, or follow up with the person outside the meeting.

By using this strategy, a facilitator sends the message to the team member that *you're important, this is important, but it's not for now*. This is important for facilitators and team members as it ensures team members know they will be heard and listened to.

However, if a facilitator promises to return to the topic later, they must follow through. Fail to do this and you're sending a message to that person that they're not as important as you said they were during the meeting.

Recording it in some way is a promise which must be honoured if relational trust is to be maintained. And relational trust is critical to maintaining the culture of psychological safety that enables all team members to feel safe and able to participate and contribute to the outcomes and processes. Of course, this strategy also contributes to the likelihood that all team members will be encouraged and committed and that their work together in the team will 'matter'.

Shifting roles

As mentioned earlier, having clarity around any team role is important. Team members need to understand that the role of the chairperson (or facilitator), is to facilitate the meeting processes. It's not about the chairperson making the ultimate decisions or telling others what they should do or think.

Sometimes this can leave the meeting facilitator feeling as though they aren't having any input or that their input is minimal because they're too occupied in implementing the actual process and managing team dynamics. What we suggest in this case is signalling your temporary change in role.

For example, if you're facilitating a meeting and you want to contribute content or add your point of view, signal this by simply saying, "Can I add something here?" Even this phrase, "Can I add something?" is invitational, because the facilitator is temporarily removing themselves from the facilitator role. You could also go one step further and physically move yourself off to the side of the team. After making your contribution, you can then return to your previous position and resume the facilitator role by saying in an approachable voice something along the lines of, "OK, let's move on." Or "How does that add to our thinking?"

If you're seated, you could signal your temporary role change by broad changes in posture – for example by leaning back or removing your glasses. These subtle shifts indicate to the team, "I'm actually shifting my role here and I'm just going to offer something as opposed to facilitating the process." In our experience we've found physical signals are essential. Without them, team members may not realise you are temporarily stepping out of your facilitator role and the process can feel less than honest. It's these micro skills that effective facilitators develop and obtain mastery in that lead to the running of increasingly effective and impactful team meetings.

Continuous, ongoing development of middle leaders

If much of the responsibility for improving student and teacher learning falls on the shoulders of middle leaders, who is looking after these team leaders and supporting them in the development of their skills to effectively facilitate team meetings? Is ongoing and targeted professional learning being provided, or is someone just told that they're the team leader and 'dumped' into the role to sink or swim?

We believe that there is a real need for professional learning and support around what the role is and isn't, which is targeted towards building team leaders' capabilities to perform the facilitation role to the highest level. This includes how to facilitate successful and impactful team meetings. It requires the establishment of school-based avenues to allow team leaders to constantly build and enhance a toolkit of skills and resources that they can draw on in the moment. For example, that could be a protocol they can use to have team members deeply reflect on a promising teaching practice, or a particular skill they might implement to handle a domineering team member at a meeting.

Unfortunately, in some schools where we have worked, we've sensed an attitude of: "You're the team leader, you deal with it." A stronger and more supportive approach is to view the development of a team leader's mastery of team meeting facilitation as a crucial component of the school's continuous improvement focus. Senior school leaders should constantly ask themselves: "How do we build the capabilities of our team leaders to do the work we are asking of them effectively?" But it's not enough to simply ask the question; every available opportunity and resource must then be commissioned to ensure that it is successfully answered.

In Summary

Help others to understand your role

Ensure that you have clarity on your role as meeting facilitator and its difference from being team leader, and help other team members to understand this, too. During a meeting, your primary role is as facilitator of process, rather than acting as the team leader, which might well be your role outside the meeting.

View the meeting as an opportunity to enhance your skills

Look at the meeting as a chance to really hone your skills as a facilitator. Yes, meetings are an opportunity to get the work done, but you can also use each agenda item as a chance to build your facilitation skills as items are worked through. You can also simultaneously take the opportunity to focus on leveraging who you are being to get the work done, and bring team members with you by being intentional about what and who being a facilitator requires you to be.

Commit to researching, developing, using and sharing facilitation strategies to improve the productivity of the team

Meetings are a professional learning opportunity for everyone involved. Every team member, whether they're a member of the school's leadership or not, should be developing similar capabilities and a common language for how to work collaboratively.

Build up a bank or toolkit of protocols

School personnel are very busy, and team leaders are probably even busier, so start to build up a toolkit of protocols and strategies that teams can use to more easily accomplish the work the team needs to undertake. When you're selecting one of these strategies or protocols from the toolkit, make sure it's relevant to either the team or the agenda item being undertaken. Choosing a strategy should be quite deliberate.

After some practise, this will become second nature. Using strategies from the toolkit depersonalises the process, which is a powerful thing. When facilitation reaches this level of mastery, team members understand that true collaboration is a disciplined process that you and they are engaged in, where everyone has the equal opportunity to have input into the decisions made. This ensures that the meeting will matter.

Taking stock:

Where is your team in relation to this essential?

Rate your team's current performance level using the following scale:

1 We're unaware of this
2 We are aware of this, but it is not yet evident in our team's practices
3 We are fully conscious of applying this
4 Automaticity – we automatically apply it in our team practice and functioning

We clearly understand the complexities of the role of facilitator.

1	2	3	4

When we act as facilitators, we are intentional in our choices of attending to the social, cognitive, physical and emotional needs of our team members.

1	2	3	4

When we act as facilitators, we use strategies like honour and divert, significance review and shifting roles to ensure the effective functioning of the team.

1	2	3	4

As a team we actively seek to grow our skills in facilitating.

1	2	3	4

How are you facilitating this action?

What might you need to stop doing, continue doing or start doing?

How does your team need to show up to increase impact and what might this mean for you as facilitator?

◇

5.
Foster Ownership

Ensure agenda items for the subsequent meeting are developed collaboratively at the current meeting

As we all know, there's the constant dilemma of never having enough time within the school day. Often there's not even enough time between meetings to develop an agenda for the next meeting, so why not just do this at the actual meeting? This approach helps build a team's ownership and commitment to the meeting and the work that is to be done during that meeting. At the end of each meeting, there should be an agenda item which could be called 'Next Meeting Agenda Items'. This item invites dialogue around the following prompt, "So as a consequence of where we got today at today's meeting, what do we need to be discussing and working on at our next meeting?"

With this approach, all team members have the chance to have legitimate input, rather than relying on the direction always coming from the team leader. Doing this also allows team members to view what they do at meetings as an ongoing process, rather than just a series of separate tasks. Where a team is implementing the action research approach, they come to recognise that each task completed at the meeting builds into this bigger process. By adopting a standard template to create the agenda for each meeting, you can use the current meeting to start building the agenda for the following meeting. This saves time and means you don't have to try to find extra time between meetings to complete this task.

This practice also gives the person allocated the facilitator role for the next meeting adequate time to research processes, protocols and strategies. It allows them to select the approach best suited to address the upcoming agenda items and engage team members in rich discussion and dialogue. As we've mentioned earlier, it's great to share this role around so that different people get the chance to learn how to facilitate the team. As the facilitator role rotates to different team members, their understanding of the team processes and their collaborative skills continues to develop.

By building the next agenda at each meeting, team members begin to strengthen their understanding of what the next logical steps for the team are. The clearer team members are about a process they are following, the more it becomes operationalised, allowing the team to implement the process with higher and higher levels of efficiency.

Developing each agenda together also allows team members to feel more included and their voices valued, as opposed to feeling "this is being done to me". We know that true collaboration is a partnership, but it is sometimes compounded by the complexities of hierarchical roles. Building the agenda together is one small way of setting up an inclusive culture that addresses this challenge to some degree. It also ensures the voices and needs of all team members are being heard, which means they're more likely to feel supported.

Successfully involving your team in developing the agenda items for the next meeting requires the team leader to have a clear understanding of the process that the team is going to implement. However, even if you're still learning the process, your understanding of the process will deepen as you lead your team members in the joint development of the meeting agenda.

It's a good idea to ensure that someone (often this becomes the role of the minute taker), is assigned the responsibility of checking the relevancy of these proposed agenda items. For example, the minute taker might ask, "How is that relevant? Does having that as an agenda item progress the work we've done at this meeting? Is that our next logical step?" This ensures that an item is not included in the agenda just because someone suggested it, but that each item is filtered through a lens to ensure it has relevance and purpose. This process also builds team members' understanding of the process the team is using.

Summary:

Make sure the agenda contains an item that requires team members to all participate in forming the agenda for the next meeting.

This practice contributes to developing mastery of meetings that matter, as it ensures all team members feel valued and can contribute. Direct involvement in determining the next steps in the team's work also deepens team members' understandings of what the team's work is, and the nuances and complexities it involves. It will also not only build their skills in understanding the team meeting process, but their involvement and commitment to the work the team does together and its important outcomes.

Taking stock:

Where is your team in relation to this essential?

Rate your team's current performance level using the following scale:

1   We're unaware of this
2   We are aware of this, but it is not yet evident in our team's practices
3   We are fully conscious of applying this
4   Automaticity – we automatically apply it in our team practice and functioning

Our team collaboratively decides on the agenda of upcoming meetings at the previous meeting.

1	2	3	4

Our team interrogates proposed agenda items to ensure relevance to our team's purpose and our shared work.

1	2	3	4

How are you facilitating this action?

What might you need to stop doing, continue doing or start doing?

How does your team need to show up to increase impact and what might this mean for you as facilitator?

$\diamond$

6.

Be on the Same Page

Ensure the actions agreed to at the meeting are clearly understood by all team members

It's vital that the actions agreed to at each meeting are clearly understood by all team members. If you've ever spoken to someone about a meeting you attended together and noted the different 'take-aways' they've drawn from the meeting, you'll know what we mean.

We all have different filters of perception, have had different experiences and understand things differently. We know from our own experience that we can present what we think in a concise and clear message to many people at the one-time - only to have just as many different interpretations of what we've said.

This is just a very human thing, but it does demonstrate the importance of making sure the actions agreed to in the meeting are clearly understood by everyone. It's the lack of clarity around actions/decisions and required follow-up outside the meeting that usually creates misunderstanding and frustration between team members. Those feelings can be poisonous to building a strong and impactful team culture of disciplined collaboration.

To minimise the risk of this happening, facilitators of effective team meetings ensure clarity and common understanding of all the agreements and decisions reached in each meeting. This can easily be achieved by a simple standing agenda item at the end of each meeting, which causes team members to consider and reflect on the commitments that have been reached. The facilitator might undertake this by saying, "Let's review the decisions we made at the meeting. Are the actions clearly understood by each of us?" It only needs to take a couple of minutes.

It is important to note that our facilitator doesn't say clearly *supported*; rather **clearly understood** by each team member. If the decisions made during the discussion of each agenda item have been made using the team's decision-making procedure, there should not, at this point, be any debate of the validity of the decisions made or action proposed. This will have already occurred. This step is designed to remind everyone of the actions agreed to and to ensure there's really no excuse for the actions not to be followed through outside the meeting.

Plan for misunderstandings

If we expect that there might be misunderstandings, then we can plan for it. One way of doing this is to ask the minute taker to summarise and record the key decisions or proposed actions at the conclusion of each agenda item, rather than waiting until the end of the meeting. The record may also include any expected follow-up and time frames.

By clearly summarising the action or decisions at the end of each agenda item, the minute taker ensures there is clarity and a common understanding among all team members. This process also helps the minute taker ensure they have accurately recorded the decision in the meeting minutes.

In practice, this might play out with the minute taker stating: "This is what I have recorded that we agreed to. This is the decision we reached. Are there any clarifying questions? No? Let's move on".

To begin with, this might feel artificial. But remember that we're talking about making the team meeting as effective and impactful as possible. We are taking a disciplined and deliberate approach to ensuring our collaborative work is of the highest quality. The way that we communicate and interact at the meeting is different to how we interact at other times, and that's because we are present at the meeting to achieve a specific outcome.

In Summary

Ensure clarity around decisions and actions

Make sure you allocate space in your meeting to review decisions that have been made, and details of time-frames and follow up, whether that be after each agenda item or at the end of the meeting.

Expect there to be misunderstandings of decisions teams reached

When we accept that each individual processes information in their own distinct and unique ways, we can plan for it. This can include asking the minute taker to summarise the key decision/s at the conclusion of each agenda item, rather than waiting until the end of the meeting.

Through this process the team may need to refine, if necessary, what is recorded on the agenda/minutes based on the quick review, reducing the chances of misunderstandings.

Allow time for clarifying questions

Make sure you allow a small window of time for team members to ask 'clarifying your understanding' questions. To maintain productivity and efficiency, this should be limited to 30 seconds per team member.

Taking stock:

Where is your team in relation to this essential?

Rate your team's current performance level using the following scale:

1   We're unaware of this
2   We are aware of this, but it is not yet evident in our team's practices
3   We are fully conscious of applying this
4   Automaticity – we automatically apply it in our team practice and functioning

We ensure we understand agreed on actions by recording them at the end of each agenda item.

1	2	3	4

We have processes in place that enable team members to freely check-in and clarify their understanding of decisions, time frames and required follow up.

1	2	3	4

How are you facilitating this action?

What might you need to stop doing, continue doing or start doing?

How does your team need to show up to increase impact and what might this mean for you as facilitator?

✦

7

Avoid Distractions

Ensure the actions agreed to at the meeting are clearly understood by all team members

It's very easy to get caught up in the *busyness* of any meeting and waste too much time on items that serve more of a general communication function. It's important to have some kind of filter, to ensure communication type items don't dominate the meeting and rob your team of time that could be spent on more crucial topics closely aligned to the team's purpose.

Of course, as anyone who's ever worked in a school knows, a lack of time is one of the biggest challenges in education. Everyone's demanding something of us, and if we are not careful, the passing on of general school communications and information can rob us of valuable time at our team meetings. Don't let these items infiltrate your meeting and consume the precious time that could better devoted to the team's core purpose –doing work that matters and makes a difference.

Remember, the entire purpose of working collaboratively is to harness the collective knowledge and intelligence of the team. So if the items on the agenda don't focus on gathering this knowledge and using that collective intelligence, then why are we allowing these items on the agenda in the first place?

We believe it pays to have a 'read only' section on your agenda, where information that simply needs to be shared with members at any time can be listed. Items listed here are really communication or information sharing items that don't need any team discussion, input, or meaning making. They don't even need to be read at the meeting. Doing this frees up more precious meeting time for higher priority agenda items.

Understand the purpose of the meeting

Having a clear understanding of the purpose of the meeting informs what will go into this 'read only' section. If team members know what the purpose of the meeting is, it becomes obvious which items should be restricted to this section.

As you think of your own meeting agendas, are there items that could be more suited to the 'read only' section? Make it everyone's responsibility to add communication items to the 'read only' part of the agenda, not just the team leader. For example, one of your team members might have attended another meeting and has some information that needs to be shared as it impacts on the work of this team. In this case, it is that team member's responsibility to add a quick summary of the relevant information in the 'read only' section. After other members have read the information provided, they can follow up with that team member outside the meeting if they have any questions.

This process ensures everyone is taking responsibility. It also supports team members by making it clearer which items should be given the highest priority at the meetings.

Make the agenda easily available

It's a great idea to allow your agenda to be easily accessed - for example online - so that it can be both read and added to before the meeting. Unfortunately, we can't guarantee team members will actually read it prior to the meeting, but at least they will not be able to claim they didn't have access to it.

Communicate the need for members to take personal responsibility

Just because something is on the meeting agenda, it doesn't necessarily mean that it's high on an individual's agenda. So make sure your team embeds the need for its members to take personal responsibility for accessing the agenda and acting on any pre-meeting preparation. It should also be the personal responsibility of each team member to follow up on any decisions or implement any actions that come out of each meeting. This may even be included as one of the norms that team members have agreed to. For example, the team may include as a specific behaviour commitment (as part of their norms) that all team members will have read the 'read only' section of the agenda prior to the meeting, and taken any action required.

Summary

Protect the work and plans of the collaborative team

Ensure that all information that may impact the integrity of the team's plans and processes is known and understood by all team members in an easy to access way.

Encourage team members to take personal responsibility for communicating such information to the team, so that team plans and processes are not derailed, nor the potential impact of the team's work reduced.

Taking stock:

Where is your team in relation to this essential?

Rate your team's current performance level using the following scale:

1   We're unaware of this
2   We are aware of this, but it is not yet evident in our team's practices
3   We are fully conscious of applying this
4   Automaticity – we automatically apply it in our team practice and functioning

Our team uses a 'read only' section to communicate information that needs to be disseminated but not discussed.

1	2	3	4

All team members may contribute items to the 'read only' section on our agenda.

1	2	3	4

Our agenda is a live document and is accessible to all.

1	2	3	4

How are you facilitating this action?

What might you need to stop doing, continue doing or start doing?

How does your team need to show up to increase impact and what might this mean for you as facilitator?

8.
Beware of Interruptions

Ensure team members are clear of any events or school happenings which might impact on the meeting's actions

Finally, ensure all team members are clear about any events or school happenings that might impact on the workings of the team. This is relevant for any school teams, and particularly for collaborative teams in a PLC implementing the action research and cycles of learning process.

Team members should have a quick and easy way of accessing (and remembering) information about any upcoming events that may impact on their team meeting or the actions which have been agreed to at the meeting. In our work with schools, we are surprised how often these things are overlooked or have been forgotten. Then suddenly someone remembers, and the work that the team has spent time planning and scheduling can't be implemented and needs to be delayed.

For example, we recently worked with a team who had put a great deal of effort into a project they wanted to implement within a certain time frame. They did all the work, talked about it and spent time making decisions. They then checked their calendar and discovered they couldn't implement their plans at their desired time because another event had already been organised and added to the calendar.

This kind of thing can be deeply frustrating and demoralising. It can also significantly impact the capacity of the team to do work that matters, and in ways that matters to the team members. So it is critically important that team members and team leaders are constantly alert to any potential disruptions to programs or plans that they have laboured so positively over. Such interruptions or obstacles can really demotivate teams. They inevitably lead to thoughts that the school leadership team doesn't really care about this work, as they haven't taken the time to keep the team informed of things that may impact upon it.

Although it's surprising how often this situation arises, it is very easily remedied. Keeping the simple calendar section on the agenda up to date ensures any such events can be worked around and also enables collaborative teams to make timelines more realistic.

As with the 'read only' section of the agenda, it should be everyone's responsibility to keep the calendar section of the agenda up to date. If someone knows there's something coming up - for example, the school camp is in July - they should take personal responsibility for adding it to the calendar to remind the rest of the team.

Summary

Protect the work and plans of the collaborative team

It is vital to ensure that all events that may impact the timing and integrity of the team's plans and programs are known and understood by all team members and accounted for in the timelines the team sets.

Individual team members should be actively encouraged to take personal responsibility for communicating such information to the team so that team plans and processes are not derailed, nor the potential impact of the team's work reduced.

This will also shore up and consolidate the team's morale and sense of collective efficacy, along with building their trust that the important work they do is valued.

It's also vital to developing the mastery of meetings that matter, as team members contribute to getting the work done (what I do), as well as looking after each other (who I am and who I need to be).

Taking stock:

Where is your team in relation to this essential?

Rate your team's current performance level using the following scale:

1 We're unaware of this
2 We are aware of this, but it is not yet evident in our team's practices
3 We are fully conscious of applying this
4 Automaticity – we automatically apply it in our team practice and functioning

Our team keeps an up-to-date 'upcoming events' section on our agenda to minimise disruptions to our work.

1	2	3	4

All team members may contribute items to the 'upcoming event' section on our agenda

1	2	3	4

How are you facilitating this action?

What might you need to stop doing, continue doing or start doing?

How does your team need to show up to increase impact and what might this mean for you as facilitator?

Epilogue

For many, becoming a teacher, or someone who leads learning, feels like a calling – a mission to serve and enable others to grow and flourish. Many educators want to ensure that future generations are educated, informed, compassionate citizens who enable each other and our planet to thrive.

Our meetings are where we talk, initiate plans, discuss options, and make decisions that determine the direction of our schools and the subsequent outcomes of our students. If we agree that education is an intrinsically noble and altruistic profession and calling, why not take as much care with our meetings? After all, they are ultimately the very foundation for the outcomes of our efforts with our students, ourselves and each other. We must dedicate ourselves to meeting the needs of the participants of our meetings as well as the organisational outcomes we pursue.

For such meetings to 'matter', they must have influence over and make a difference to participants, beneficiaries and all those impacted. They must be very carefully and intentionally planned, prepared for, facilitated, engaged in and followed up. And for the work to be 'done' collaboratively, we need to bring people with us and engage their hearts, minds and spirits, while meeting their social, emotional cognitive and physical needs. We need to show our people that we see them as human beings who want to make a contribution to something important. As a result, we do whatever we can to ensure that they can make that contribution and find meaning in their work lives.

For us, effective or successful meetings take minimum time and produce maximum impact on student and educator learner, whilst generating genuine team member engagement and satisfaction. They focus on both *what I do* and *who I am*, in both the meeting space and in the team.

The ultimate goal of any school meeting should be to serve as the work engine of school improvement. It's all about progressing the core mission of any school - to continuously improve student learning.

We hope the eight essentials we've covered will help you build a thriving collaborative culture with your team. We trust they'll support you to facilitate highly effective and impactful meetings within your school that truly make a difference to students, teachers and your community.

And we hope that by developing mastery of these essentials, you will show your people that you care about and believe in them, that you value and welcome their contributions, and that you want them to find meaning in their professional lives.

Indeed, through mastery of meetings that matter and our collaborative endeavours, we will forge more meaningful connections with our colleagues and help to ignite the human potential of the students and communities we serve.

Reference List

Aguilar, E. (2016). *The Art of Coaching Teams. Building Resilient Communities That Transform Schools.* Jossey-Bass: San Francisco, CA.

Combs, J. (2019). *What is dialogue?* University of Dayton Blogs, Monday October 28, 2019, Available at < https://udayton.edu/blogs/dialoguezone/19-10-28-what-is-dialogue.php>

Danvers, J., De Blasio, H. & Grift, G. (2020). *Five Ways of Being. What Learning Leaders Think, Do and Say Every Day.* Hawker Brownlow: Moorabbin, AUS.

Du Four, R., Du Four, R., Eaker R., Many, T. W. & Mattos, M. (with Grift,G., & Sloper, C.). (2019). *Concise answers to frequently asked questions about Professional Learning Communities At Work® (Rev. Australian ed.).* Hawker Brownlow: Moorabbin, AUS

Garmston, R. J. & Wellman, B. M. (2013). *The Adaptive School. A Sourcebook for Developing Collaborative Groups 2ed.* Hawker Brownlow: Moorabbin, AUS

Hirsh, S., Delehant, A., & Sparks, S. (1994). *Keys to Successful Meetings.* Oxford, OH: National Staff Development Council.

Lipton, L. & Wellman, B.M. (2016). Groups At Work: Strategies and structures for professional learning. MiraVia, LLC

Oxford Languages, (n.d.) Discussion. Available at <https://www.google.com/search?q=discussion+meaning&oq=discussion+meaning&aqs=chrome..69i57j0i512l9.2943j1j15&sourceid=chrome&ie=UTF-8>

Sloper, C. & Grift. G. (2020). *Collaborative Teams That Work.* Hawker Brownlow: Moorabbin, AUS.